THEIR NAMES TO LIVE

What the VIETNAM VETERANS MEMORIAL Means to America

Brent Ashabranner

Photographs by Jennifer Ashabranner

Twenty-First Century Books
Brookfield, Connecticut

To Colleen Carney Shine

Library of Congress Cataloging-in-Publication Data
Ashabranner, Brent K., 1921–
Their names to live: what the Vietnam Veterans Memorial means to
America/Brent Ashabranner: photographs by Jennifer Ashabranner.
p.   cm.
Includes bibliographical references (p.   ) and index.
Summary: Describes the planning and creation of the Vietnam Vet-
erans Memorial and how it came to be a symbol for the dead of all
American wars.
ISBN 0-7613-3235-9 (lib. bdg.)
1. Vietnam Veterans Memorial (Washington, D.C.)—Juvenile
literature.   [1. Vietnam Veterans Memorial (Washington, D.C.)
2. National monuments.]   I. Ashabranner, Jennifer, ill.   II. Title.
DS559.83.W18A86   1998
959.704'36—dc21   98-21004   CIP   AC

Published by Twenty-First Century Books
A division of The Millbrook Press, Inc.
2 Old New Milford Road
Brookfield, Connecticut 06804

CONTENTS

Their bodies are buried in peace;
but their names liveth for evermore.
Ecclesiasticus XLIV, 14

Ten years ago my daughter Jennifer and I collaborated on a book that we called *Always to Remember*. It was a book we believed in and loved, and it told the remarkable story of the creation of the Vietnam Veterans Memorial and the people responsible for its creation. In the years that have passed, the memorial has gained a unique place in the hearts and minds of the American people. In *Their Names to Live*, our purpose has been to tell the story, in words and photographs, of how and why the Vietnam Veterans Memorial has come to mean so much to our country.

In Chapter Two, I have adapted material from *Always to Remember* that is especially relevant to the story we tell in *Their Names to Live*.

Brent Ashabranner

On November 13, 1982, the Vietnam Veterans Memorial was dedicated in Washington, D.C. A huge crowd of more than 150,000, mostly Vietnam War veterans from all over the country, gathered on the grassy slopes around the memorial at its location on the Mall between the Washington Monument and

THE VIETNAM VETERANS MEMORIAL (left and right) *is firmly anchored in the heart of American history. The eastern wing stretches toward the Washington Monument, the western wing toward the Lincoln Memorial, both beloved symbols of our country's heritage.*

the Lincoln Memorial. For many, it was their first look at the wall of polished black granite bearing the names of 57,939 American servicemen and women killed or missing in the Vietnam War.

The dedication began at 2:00 P.M., and Air Force Chaplain Owen J. Hendry clearly was thinking of the names carved on the memorial when he gave the invocation: "Your presence is felt in this place as a mighty wind, O God, echoing again the words once spoken by your prophet Isaiah, 'I have called you by name, you are mine.' Keep them close to you, O God, in your eternal peace."

The main speaker at the dedication was Senator John Warner of Virginia. His message was blunt and clear: "We Americans must face the sober lessons of history. We learned a terrible lesson from the Vietnam War—a lesson we must never forget. We learned that we should never again ask our men and women to serve in a war which we do not intend to win. We

VISITORS SEE THEMSELVES
and other visitors in the memorial's polished black granite. They are drawn into it and, in a haunting way, become a part of the wall of names.

SINCE ITS DEDICATION, *the Vietnam Veterans Memorial has become one of the most visited memorials in Washington, D.C.*

learned that we should not enter a war unless it is necessary for our national survival. We learned that, if we do enter such a war, we must support our men and women to the fullest extent of our powers."

MANY VISITORS *feel compelled to touch a name on the wall, even if they did not know anyone whose name is there.*

In less than an hour, the formal ceremonies ended with the vast gathering singing "God Bless America." Master of Ceremonies Jan C. Scruggs went to the microphone and said simply, "Ladies and Gentlemen, the Vietnam Veterans Memorial is now dedicated."

After a hushed moment, a great cheer arose, and thousands of people surged forward. Some wept as they stared at the wall of names. Some found the name of a husband, a father, a friend, a battle comrade and touched it. Some placed flowers, messages, and other tokens of love at the bases of the panels. In that November moment what has sometimes been called "wall magic" was born.

I was not at the dedication of the Vietnam Veterans Memorial, but I have seen and felt wall magic countless times since that historic day. I have seen it as my reflection in the polished black granite becomes a part of the wall of names. I once felt it when I read a note taped to a scuffed baseball placed beneath one of the memorial panels: "Teddy, people still talk about your fastball. Mom and I are always thinking about you. Dad." Wall magic is in the special message that the memorial holds for each viewer.

THE AUTHOR *experiences the wall's haunting reflective power.*

TWO: A NATION CONFUSED AND DIVIDED

The Vietnam War ended in 1975, only seven years before the Vietnam Veterans Memorial was built and dedicated. The war bitterly divided America. Millions of Americans believed that our support of non-Communist South Vietnam was necessary to keep communism from growing in Southeast Asia. But millions of other Americans believed the United States should never have been fighting a war in Asia. They felt that we had no business interfering in what they considered a Vietnamese internal matter. Whether all of Vietnam became Communist, they contended, was for the Vietnamese to decide, no matter what the United States thought of the decision.

If U.S. military forces had stayed in Vietnam only a short time, these differing points of view might not have hardened the way they did. But the Vietnam War was not short. To the contrary, it became the longest war in United States history, and the number of American troops in Vietnam steadily increased. By 1967, the number reached half a million. Still North Vietnam's fighting forces in South Vietnam remained strong, and the deadly guerrilla war in jungles and rice paddies did not slacken. Americans were fighting and dying, but victory was nowhere in sight.

U.S. military leaders continued to insist that the war was winnable and asked for still more troops to be sent to Vietnam. But increasing numbers of Americans believed that Vietnam had become a bottomless pit for American troops and equipment. By 1967, massive antiwar demonstrations were taking place in the United States.

President Lyndon Johnson was unwilling to further increase troop strength in Vietnam, but he was unable to find a way to end the war without admitting defeat. In what amounted to an admission of failure, he announced that he would not seek reelection as president. Richard Nixon, who succeeded Johnson as president, said he had a plan to end the war that would bring the United States "peace with honor."

But the war went on for more than four years after President Nixon took office. Finally, in 1973, a cease-fire agreement was signed. Most U.S. forces returned home. In April 1975, the Army of North Vietnam, ignoring the cease-fire, invaded South Vietnam and quickly defeated the South Vietnamese Army. The few remaining American armed forces and embassy staff made a last-minute escape from Vietnam. The Communist North Vietnamese had taken over the country. At last the war was over.

The cost of the war to the United States was staggering. More than 58,000 men and women were killed or missing. More than 300,000 were wounded, 74,000 of them crippled with a more than 50 percent disability. In excess of $140 billion had been spent on the war. There were other costs in shattered or permanently marred lives.

The United States had never before lost a war. Even after the war ended, disagreement continued about what should or should not have happened. With that disagreement came a loss of national confidence and common purpose that the American people had never before experienced.

Another tragic outcome of the war was the treatment of veterans upon their return to America. The veterans of earlier American wars had been welcomed home as heroes, with ticker-tape parades, speeches of praise, and the friendly smiles and support of everyone who saw them in uniform. Not so with the veterans of the Vietnam War. America was sick of the cost and dissension of a war it did not win. Most Vietnam veterans were at best ignored; many met outright hostility.

Dazed, hurt, unappreciated, unable to communicate, the men and women who fought in Vietnam were by any definition casualties of the war.

In that climate of rejection, the idea of building a memorial to those who had served and died in Vietnam seemed unthinkable, even absurd. But it was not unthinkable to Jan Scruggs. He was nineteen in 1969 when he joined the army and was sent to Vietnam, assigned to the 199th Light Infantry Brigade. He was in Vietnam for more than a year, and in that time he saw more than half of his company killed or wounded. Scruggs himself was wounded and decorated for gallantry.

After returning from Vietnam, Scruggs went to college and earned two degrees. But even when he was deep in his studies, thoughts of Vietnam would not go away. At American University in Washington, D.C., the idea of a Vietnam Veterans Memorial first came to him. America wanted to forget the Vietnam War, but he thought it shouldn't forget. A memorial to the men and women who lost their lives in Vietnam would help the country remember. And maybe, Scruggs thought, a memorial might help lessen the war bitterness that still divided Americans. But at the time those were only the thoughts and dreams of a college student.

In early 1979, married and working for the U.S. Department of Labor, Jan Scruggs saw a movie called *The Deer Hunter*. It is a powerful story of Americans in the Vietnam

War. The movie upset Scruggs, shook him badly. After he got home from the theater, he couldn't sleep. He stayed up most of the night, and scenes of his own Vietnam experiences began to flash in his head.

"It was just like I was in the army again and I saw my buddies dead there," Scruggs said years later. "Twelve guys, their brains and intestines all over the place. Twelve guys in a pile where the mortar rounds had come in."

The morning after that night of awful memories, Scruggs told his wife that he was going to build a memorial to all of the men and women who had been killed in Vietnam and that all their names would be on it.

"I became obsessed," Scruggs said.

People told him that his idea wouldn't work. They said the war was still too much an emotional issue for people to support a memorial. The government would never approve the money for it. Besides, memorials can't be rushed. The Washington Monument took a hundred years to complete. The Lincoln Memorial wasn't finished until fifty years after Lincoln's death.

Scruggs listened to the objections, but he had answers. He didn't intend to build a memorial to the Vietnam War but rather to the men and women who fought and died in the war. There was a big difference. And Scruggs didn't want government money. As he saw it, the money would come from private citizens all over the country. As for taking fifty years to build— well, that just couldn't happen. The memorial was needed now.

Two men, Robert Doubek and John Wheeler, did listen to Scruggs, and they did not tell him his idea was impossible. Both Doubek and Wheeler were Washington lawyers, and both had served as officers in Vietnam. Doubek showed Scruggs how to form a Vietnam Veterans Memorial Fund that could develop plans for the memorial and receive tax-exempt contributions. Wheeler knew a wide range of influential people whom he encouraged to support the memorial plan.

Scruggs knew nothing about holding a press conference, but he held one anyway to announce that a memorial to the men and women who had served and died in Vietnam would be built. He asked for support and money from private citizens. Many people wrote praising the idea, but after a month the Vietnam Veterans Memorial Fund had received only $144.50 in contributions. Television news commentators and comedians made jokes about the financial "support" the memorial idea was receiving.

But the joke proved to be on them. Scruggs, Doubek, and Wheeler continued their tireless efforts. Out of an endless round of meetings came capable volunteers for the publicity, fund-raising, and other tasks of the Vietnam Veterans Memorial Fund. Valuable supporters in the business and professional worlds were found.

Before a Vietnam Veterans Memorial could be built on public land in Washington, D.C., the Senate and House of Representatives had to pass a bill approving such a memorial, and the president had to sign it. As a Maryland citizen, Jan Scruggs went to see the senior senator from Maryland, Charles Mathias. Senator Mathias had opposed American involvement in Vietnam during the years of conflict, but the senator was able to distinguish between the war and those who fought it. He became a leading supporter of the memorial in Congress.

In the end, the bill passed both houses of Congress unanimously, and on July 1, 1980, President Jimmy Carter signed it into law. The bill said that the Vietnam Veterans Memorial should be built on the Mall near the Lincoln Memorial. In his most optimistic dreams, Jan Scruggs had never thought that such a location was possible.

Now Scruggs and his team had to finish collecting the money to build the memorial. Some wealthy Americans, such as Texas billionaire H. Ross Perot and Senator John Warner, made large contributions. But finally it was thousands of ordinary Americans, sending amounts of $1, $5, $10, and $20, who donated most of the more than $8 million needed to build the memorial.

One thing the law authorizing a Vietnam Veterans Memorial did not mention was what the memorial should look like; that decision was left to the Vietnam Veterans Memorial Fund. But Scruggs, Doubek, and Wheeler knew nothing about designing memorials. They knew it should be something that would bring the divided American people closer together. And Scruggs insisted that the name of every American man and woman killed or missing in the war had to be on it. But they had no idea what the design should be.

The answer, they decided, was to hold a national design competition open to all Americans. The winning design would receive a prize of $20,000, but the real prize would be the winner's knowledge that the memorial would become a part of American history on the Mall in Washington, D.C. A panel of well-known architects, landscape architects, sculptors, and designers was chosen to decide the winner.

Announcement of the competition in October 1980 brought an astonishing response. The Vietnam Veterans Memorial Fund received more than five thousand inquiries from every state in the nation. As expected, architects and sculptors were especially interested. Everyone who inquired received a booklet explaining the criteria. Among the most important: the memorial must honor the memory of those Americans who served and died in the Vietnam War; it must contain the names of all persons killed or missing in action; it must be in harmony with its location on the Mall. Everyone was sent photographs of the Mall location where the memorial was to be built.

The competitors were given three months to prepare their designs, and within that time limit 1,421 designs were submitted—a record for that kind of design competition. When the designs were spread out for jury selection, they filled a large airplane hangar. The jury spent one week reviewing the designs, and on May 1 made its report to the Vietnam Veterans Memorial Fund. The experts declared Entry 1,026 the winner. The report called it "the finest and most appropriate" of all submitted and said it was "superbly harmonious" with the site on the Mall.

When the name of the winner was revealed, the art and architecture worlds were stunned. The name was not that of a nationally famous architect or sculptor. The creator of Entry 1,026 was a twenty-one-year-old student at Yale University. Her name—unknown as yet in any field of art or architecture—was Maya Lin.

How could this be? How could an undergraduate student win one of the most important design competitions ever held? Who was Maya Lin?

Reporters soon discovered that Maya Lin was a Chinese-American young woman who had been born and raised in the small midwestern city of Athens, Ohio. Her father, Henry Haun Lin, was dean of fine arts at Ohio University, and her mother, Julia L. Lin, was a professor of Oriental and English literature. Maya Lin's parents were born to culturally prominent families in China. But with the power of communism growing in China in the late 1940s, they left the country and came to the United States. They met and married in their new homeland.

MAYA LIN *at First Day ceremony for a Vietnam Veterans Memorial commemorative stamp issued by the United States Post Office on November 10, 1984. Others in picture* (from left): *Brigadier General George Price, Postmaster General William F. Bolger, Jan Scruggs, John Wheeler.* (CREDIT: CAROLOU MARQUET)

Maya Lin grew up in an atmosphere of art and literature, but she went to Yale without a clear idea of what she wanted to study. In time she decided to major in Yale's undergraduate program in architecture. The professor in one of her classes thought that having his students prepare a design of the proposed Vietnam Veterans Memorial would be a worthwhile course assignment.

Maya Lin and two of her classmates decided to visit Washington to look at the Mall site where the memorial was to be built. When they arrived, Maya Lin remembers, Constitution Gardens was awash with a late November sun; the park was full of light, alive with joggers and people walking beside the park's lake.

"It was while I was at the site that I designed it," Maya Lin said later in an interview about the memorial. "It just popped into my head. It was a beautiful park. I didn't want to destroy a living park. . . .When I looked at the site I just knew I wanted something horizontal that took you in, that made you feel safe within the park, yet at the same time reminding you of the dead. So I just imagined opening up the earth. . . ."

When Maya Lin returned to Yale, she made a clay model of the vision that had come to her in Constitution Gardens. Her professor liked her conception and encouraged her to enter the competition. She put her design on paper, a task that took six weeks, and mailed it to Washington. And the rest is history.

But at first the history was not untroubled. The Vietnam Veterans Memorial Fund accepted Maya Lin's design; but when photographs of it were published, some veterans and others who had strongly supported the idea of a memorial simply did not like or understand Maya Lin's memorial design. They called it "unheroic" and "a black gash of shame." Why not use white marble instead of black granite? they asked. Why not build it aboveground instead of burying it in the earth? Why not build a memorial showing some of the heroic actions of Vietnam servicemen and women?

Maya Lin was hurt by the criticism, but she said, "I hope they will give it a chance and not close their minds."

Construction of the memorial could not begin without the approval of the secretary of the interior, and Secretary James Watt refused to give his approval while there was still strong opposition to the memorial's design. After months of bitter argument, a compromise was reached. The opponents of Maya Lin's design would withdraw their objections if a statue of American soldiers was added to the memorial. Secretary Watt gave his approval.

GENERAL COLIN POWELL, *then Chairman of the Joint Chiefs of Staff, delivered the main speech at the 1991 Memorial Day ceremonies.*

THE STATUE *of three servicemen, the work of sculptor Frederick Hart, is a part of the Vietnam Veterans Memorial. Although realistic to the smallest detail, the realism does not detract from Maya Lin's abstract memorial design. By an inspired placement of the statue, the three men seem to have emerged from a clump of trees atop the hill above the wall. They have sighted the black wall in the distance and seem to be looking at the names inscribed there.*

THE MEMORIAL *has become an emotional meeting place for Vietnam War veterans.*

Groundbreaking ceremonies were held on March 26, 1982. Many emotional speeches were made, but the words of Army Chaplain Max D. Sullivan surely came closest to expressing the hopes of Jan Scruggs, Robert Doubek, John Wheeler, and many others when he said: "May this be a holy place of healing for the conflicting emotions of that terrible, divisive war. . . ."

Shovels bit into the earth. The ground was broken. The building of the Vietnam Veterans Memorial had begun.

THREE: VETERANS DAY

On a cool November day, I went once more to the Vietnam Veterans Memorial. I long ago lost count of the number of times I have been there, but this day, Veterans Day, the eleventh day of November, has always been the day I like best to visit the memorial. Veterans Day honors all persons who

COLOR GUARD, *Veterans Day, November 11, 1997*

have served in our country's armed forces, both in times of peace and times of war. But this day at the Vietnam Veterans Memorial is most special for the 2.5 million American men and women who served in that distant Asian country. It is truly their day.

On this day, the fourteenth anniversary of the memorial's dedication, I arrived about midmorning. Thousands of people were already at the wall and on the hill above, around the bronze statues of the soldiers and the recently added Vietnam Women's Memorial. Many of the morning visitors were dressed in their Vietnam service uniforms or wore jackets denoting their Vietnam experience. I passed a tall, lean man dressed in the camouflage combat uniform of the Marine Corps. A gray-haired man wore a jacket that said: A BAND OF BROTHER'S [sic] IA DRANG VALLEY VIETNAM 65. Several men

HEAVY FIGHTING *took place in 1965-1966 in the South Vietnam central highlands' Ia Drang Valley. In a campaign called Operation Crazy Horse, the U.S. first Cavalry Division decisively defeated North Vietnamese Communist forces.*

wore the green berets of the Special Forces, and here and there I saw a red beret worn by the American servicemen who had trained the Vietnamese Ranger units. An army nurse looked at a name on one of the panels where the wings of the memorial come together.

There had been a time in which few of these men and women would have worn the clothes they wore today, the first years after the war when the nation turned its back on them. I recalled the words of former senator George McGovern. He was a bitter critic of the Vietnam War, but speaking of the Vietnam veterans, he once said: "I was treated as a hero when I got home from World War II, but I was not any braver than those who served in Vietnam, and we almost sneaked them in under cover of darkness."

The Vietnam Veterans Memorial changed all that. Now the veterans of that war wore their service uniforms and insignia proudly.

And McGovern was right about the bravery of those who fought in Vietnam: 24 percent of all Marines who were sent into battle in Vietnam were killed or wounded. That is the highest casualty rate in Marine Corps history.

Every day is a day of memories at the Vietnam Veterans Memorial, but the remembrances on Veterans Day often have a special flavor. As I walked from the east wing to the west toward the Lincoln Memorial, I saw worn combat boots, a Purple Heart, a battered canteen, an Airborne shoulder insignia pinned to a note with a woman's signature. The Purple Heart made me think about the corporal who was awarded the Silver Star for his heroism in the Desert Storm Gulf War. He brought his medal to the wall and left it beneath a panel on which his father's name was engraved. Attached to the medal was a simple message: "To Dad, Love, Your Son."

A NATIVE AMERICAN (left) *places a sacred sage bundle beside a name on the wall. More than 250 Native Americans from many tribes died in the Vietnam War.*

A CANADIAN FLAG (right) *at the memorial on Veterans Day. About thirty thousand Canadians— sometimes called "the unknown veterans"—joined the U.S. armed forces and fought in the Vietnam War.*

The Vietnam Women's Memorial was dedicated in November 1993, and I had not yet seen it, so I went there this morning, walking up the path that circles the statue of the soldiers and leads to the new memorial a short distance away. When the women's memorial had been proposed, fears were expressed that still another statue near the Vietnam Veterans Memorial might be distracting and take away from the power of the great black wall.

I understood that concern, but now, seeing the Vietnam Women's Memorial for the first time, I felt reassured. The bronze statue of the servicewomen sits in a small grove of trees

MANY WORN COMBAT BOOTS, *a traditional symbol of warfare, have been left at the memorial since its dedication.*

A TRIBUTE *to U.S. Army dogs left at the wall on Veterans Day*

on a ridge above the grassy slope that descends to the wall. The new memorial is easily accessible to visitors but seems enclosed in a setting of privacy. The wall can be seen at the bottom of the hill, but for me there was no sense that the women's memorial is trying to intrude on it.

The women's statue is the work of sculptor Glenna Goodacre. It depicts a nurse holding a wounded soldier. Another servicewoman anxiously scans the sky for an evacuation helicopter. A third kneels to pick up the fallen soldier's helmet. The dark bronze statue is charged with emotion, and I

think it does exactly what the backers of a women's memorial wanted it to do. It makes a clear statement about the dedicated service and compassion of the women who served in Vietnam, and it does so without any glorification of war.

General Colin Powell spoke at the ground breaking ceremony of the Vietnam Women's Memorial on July 29, 1993. He said that more than 265,000 women served in uniform during the Vietnam War and 11,500 of them served in Vietnam.

"The nurses saw the bleakest, most terrifying face of war," the general said, "the mangled men, the endless sobs of wounded kids . . . not just now and then, but day after day, night after hellish night." And General Powell concluded by saying that the memorial would "celebrate the hope and the strength, the tenderness and the power, the kindness and the passion" of American women who served in Vietnam.

On this Veterans Day a steady stream of visitors came to the Vietnam Women's Memorial. Many of the women visitors were in military uniforms; some wore ribbons identifying them as Red Cross workers with Vietnam service. A woman sitting on one of the benches around the memorial wore green fatigues. The red lettering on the back of her jacket said DONUT DOLLY and gave the dates of her service in Vietnam. A number of visitors brought flowers, wreaths, notes, and memorabilia to place around the statue.

When I left, it was with a feeling that the Vietnam Women's Memorial had succeeded in its purpose of recognizing the service and sacrifice of a group of American women who had been too little recognized for many years.

AMERICAN RED CROSS *workers carried out an eleven-year program of assistance in Vietnam during the war, helping in military hospitals in many ways. More than six hundred young women college graduates served in Red Cross teams to bring recreational programs— and cookies and donuts— to American troops. Affectionately known as "Donut Dollies," they traveled by truck, Jeep, helicopter, and plane to reach isolated military bases.*

The outpouring of messages and mementos left at the Vietnam Veterans Memorial is unique; no other national memorial has evoked such a response. On special days the tokens of love and remembrance are many, on rainy or snowy days perhaps only a few, but I have never been to the memorial when there were none.

I am sometimes puzzled by the mementos left, sometimes deeply touched, always reminded that behind the names on the memorial there were and are mothers, fathers, wives, children, grandchildren, friends, and sweethearts who still love and miss those who did not return from Vietnam. What is the meaning of a tattered dollar bill beneath panel 24E? An empty red glass beneath panel 14W? A can of sardines, a teddy bear, Tinker Toys, a soccer ball beneath other panels? Only the person who brought the remembrance can know what it means to him or her and what it would have meant to a special name on the wall.

Notes and letters left at the memorial are different. You understand, at least in part, the emotion behind them. And I remember a card left at the wall by a woman whose husband's name was on one of the black granite panels. She had put the card there on what would have been their silver wedding anniversary—twenty-five years. It reminded me of how long

MANY TEDDY BEARS *have been left at the wall since the memorial's dedication.*

CHRISTMAS MEMORIES

the Vietnam War had been over—and of how long the important memories are part of our lives.

I long ago decided it was all right to read the messages left at the memorial. They are expressions of private grief and love, but I think that the people who leave them do not mind sharing their thoughts and feelings with others; perhaps they want to share them.

More than 55,000 remembrances of all kinds have been left at the wall since it was dedicated, and that number does not include tens of thousands of flowers, wreaths, and other floral arrangements. Organic material is not saved, but National Park Service rangers collect all other items left at the memorial. The remembrances are gathered up at the end of each day and sent to a warehouse known as the Museum Resource Center. At the center every item collected gets a bar code and is placed in a plastic bag.

David Guynes, former director of the center, once said to me: "There are so many questions, so many mysteries, in these memorabilia. So many stories are in them, so much feeling, emotion, heartache. What can be learned about America and Americans from these things they have brought? Altogether, these materials make up a very important part of the story of the Vietnam War. This is the material of social history."

Duery Felton, curator of the National Vietnam Veterans Collection at the Museum Resource Center, told me that the number of memorabilia and messages being left at the wall is increasing on special days. During one three-day period in

THOUSANDS *of personnel who served in Vietnam returned home only to die as a result of physical or emotional wounds received during their tour of duty. The Friends of the Vietnam Veterans Memorial has a program that honors eligible persons.*

1997—Memorial Day, the day before, and the day after—park rangers collected 2,300 items that had been left at the wall.

And yet, in a certain sense, each of the thousands of things left at the memorial is unique. The reason, of course, is that the person who left it and the person whose name is on the wall had a relationship that was theirs alone.

Father's Day, the third Sunday of each June, has always been a special day at the Vietnam Veterans Memorial. Since 1991, it has become most special. That year the Friends of the Vietnam Veterans Memorial began a Father's Day program of placing a rose and a message beneath a name on the wall for anyone, any-where in the country, who asks them to do so. There is no fee, not even for the cost of the rose.

Early on Father's Day morning a group of Friends volun-teers gathers in a circle near the memorial; each volunteer is

BOTH WINGS *of the memorial are lined with hundreds of red and yellow roses on Father's Day. Red roses are for those whose deaths have been confirmed, yellow roses for those still listed as missing.*

A VOLUNTEER
touches the name with the rose before reading the message.

A YOUNG VOLUNTEER
helps on Father's Day.

given an armful of roses with messages attached to them. A name and panel designation are on each rose. After a prayer, the volunteers walk single file down the path in front of the wall. Each person goes to his or her task quickly, finding the proper panel, taking a rose and touching it to the name for which it is intended, then reading aloud the message attached to the rose. The rose is then placed at the base of the panel.

On the most recent Father's Day, Jennifer was at the memorial taking photographs. As she walked along the wall, she noticed one of the volunteers whose young son—he was perhaps six—was helping carry the roses.

"This is fun," Jennifer heard the boy say.

"Yes," his father agreed. "It is fun to help make people feel good."

NAMES TO LIVE • FIVE: THEIR NAMES
FIVE: THEIR NAMES TO LIVE • FIVE:
THEIR NAMES TO LIVE • FIVE: THEIR
LIVE • FIVE: THEIR NAMES TO LIVE
THEIR NAMES TO LIVE • FIVE: THEIR
VE: THEIR NAMES TO LIVE • FIVE: TH
TO LIVE • FIVE: THEIR NAMES TO LIVE

FIVE: THEIR NAMES TO LIVE

Through the names, the Memorial speaks to us. Its message is both simple and profound: "Look deeply into my black granite face, and see yourself in the reflection—your face superimposed on the names. Never forget the names, the names, the names for they hold the answer."
Terrence O'Donnell,
Former U.S. Air Force officer in Vietnam

When all else has been said, the overpowering magic of the Vietnam Veterans Memorial is in the names and in the way the visitor experiences them. The stone walkway in front of the memorial is only ten feet wide, so you are always near the names on the wall. The panels of the memorial rise in height as they stretch toward the center. The first small panels contain only a few names; you see them, but you don't really *feel* them. But as the path descends, the names grow in number. Suddenly you look at the black granite wall and you see nothing but names, a wall of names, each name different, each one representing a life cut short by war. You stare at the names, almost hypnotized. When you first heard that the memorial contains more than 58,000 names of the dead and missing in the Vietnam War, it was just a number. You could not comprehend it.

"THESE NAMES, *seemingly infinite in number . . ."* Maya Lin

Now, looking at the wall, you know what 58,000 means, and you are overwhelmed by the meaning.

"I wept," said writer James J. Kilpatrick, describing the first time he saw the wall of names. "The memorial carries a message for all ages: this is what war is all about."

The arrangement of the names on the wall helps you understand the human tragedy of war. The names are not alphabetical. They are not organized by branch of service. They are not arranged by rank. A private's name may be next to a colonel's. The names appear on the wall in the time sequence in which the person was killed or declared missing. The years 1959 to 1975 cover a seeming eternity of days— almost six thousand—on which young Americans died.

I once heard a veteran say, "I know twelve names in a row up there. One night, one fight." He was staring at one of the tall black panels.

A FRIENDS *of the Vietnam Veterans Memorial volunteer* (left) *helps a visitor trace a name.*

TRACING A NAME

Behind every name on the memorial was a life that ended before it should have ended. That is what the wall of names tells us every time we see it, and that is what we can never get used to. After *Always to Remember* was published, many people wrote or told me about names on the wall. I cannot forget those names, not a single one, and whenever I go to the memorial my eyes will inevitably seek out some of them.

Brian J. O'Callaghan. Brian and Ginger leaving
Andrews Air Force Base chapel on a very happy day.

BRIAN J. O'CALLAGHAN
Panel 14W, Line 39
First Lieutenant, Army.
Date of Birth: June 30, 1945.
Date of Casualty: January 16, 1970.
Home of Record: Alexandria, Virginia.

"He was a fun-loving guy."

That is the way Ginger Lonergan remembers Brian O'Callaghan, her former husband. They met on a blind date when he was a student at the University of Virginia and she was attending Radford College, a Virginia girls' school. He was an enthusiastic dancer, liked to be around people having a good time, and especially enjoyed a lively party.

Brian was a good student at the university, although he didn't start out that way. He had trouble with his grades in his freshman year, no doubt because he liked having fun so much, and dropped out of school for a year. When he came back to the university, he was serious about his studies and did excellent work in his political science major. He knew that he wanted to be a lawyer and passed the qualifying test for entrance into the University of Virginia law school.

The conflict in Vietnam was raging at its greatest intensity during the mid-sixties when Brian was at the university. Like millions of other young Americans, Brian questioned the moral right of the United States to be in Vietnam and the necessity of the war to our national interests. But he never thought of leaving the country—going to Canada or Sweden—as many young men did to avoid the draft. What Brian did in order to finish his bachelor's degree was join the Reserve Officers' Training Corps (ROTC) at the university.

Almost immediately after graduation Brian was placed on active army duty with the rank of second lieutenant. He and Ginger were married on October 27, 1968, but soon Brian was sent to Panama for jungle combat training. After Panama he was assigned to Fort Hood in Texas, and Ginger was able to go with him. Ginger remembers that on the way to Fort Hood, they stopped in New Orleans for two days to enjoy that city's preparations for Mardi Gras. Brian still liked to have fun.

By October 1969, Brian, now a first lieutenant, was in Vietnam, assigned as a platoon commander in Company C, First Battalion, Sixty-ninth Armor, Fourth Infantry Division. On January 8, less than three months after he arrived, Company C was in battle, carrying out an assault on a hill crucial to the safety of a U.S. landing zone. Brian's platoon came under heavy fire from antitank rockets, mortars, and small arms. Brian was critically wounded and was flown by helicopter to a field hospital. He died at the hospital on January 16 without ever regaining consciousness.

After his death, Brian was awarded the Silver Star for gallantry, and this portion of the award citation tells graphically what happened that January 8 on Hill 564:

> When one of his tanks was immobilized and the safety of
> its crew jeopardized, Lieutenant O'Callaghan maneu-
> vered his vehicle into a fighting support position to shield

and protect the disabled vehicle. As Lieutenant O'Callaghan was effecting emergency recovery procedures, his vehicle received a direct hit, seriously wounding him. Refusing medical attention, Lieutenant O'Callaghan remained with the disabled vehicle until it was moved to safety, and continued to direct operations and engage the enemy until he was mortally wounded. First Lieutenant O'Callaghan's extraordinary courage, determination and exemplary devotion to duty are in keeping with the highest traditions of the military service and reflect great credit upon him, his unit and the United States Army.

Ginger, who today teaches autistic children at an elementary school in Fairfax County, Virginia, has only one good memory from the heartbreaking days following Brian's death. After the return of his body and his burial in a small Quaker cemetery near Washington, D.C., Ginger received this letter:

Dear Mrs. O'Callaghan:

We, the men of the 1st Platoon, Company C, 1st Battalion 69th Armor (the tank platoon your husband commanded) have a request to make of you. We have enclosed a money order for $110, which was voluntarily given by the men in your husband's platoon. It is their request that you place this amount with a florist of your choice and have flowers placed on Lieutenant O'Callaghan's place of rest each week until the amount is used up.

We send you our deepest sympathy and our most sincere prayers for a departed comrade.

Homer L. Hunt
Platoon Sargent, 1st Platoon
Company C, 1st Bn, 69th Armor

Brian O'Callaghan was a fun-loving guy who wondered why his country should be fighting a war in Vietnam. But he went there when he had to and, when he had to, he fought and died like a hero.

DAN BULLOCK

Panel 23W, Line 96
Private First Class, Marine Corps.
Date of Birth: December 12, 1949.
Date of Casualty: June 6, 1969.
Home of Record: New York City.

The information above is all that is provided in the directory of names at the Vietnam Veterans Memorial. Official Marine Corps records give some additional details about Dan Bullock: He was eighteen years old when he enlisted in the Marines on September 18, 1968, nineteen when he died. In Vietnam he was assigned to Company F, Second Battalion, Fifth Marine Regiment, a part of the First Marine Division. While he was on night-guard duty at An Hoa Combat Base in Quang Nam Province, the base came under heavy hostile ground attack. Dan was killed by multiple small-arms fire.

Dan Bullock would seem to be just another tragic statistic of a tragic war. The average age of all Americans who died in Vietnam was nineteen. But statistics seldom tell all the story, and sometimes they do not tell any of it.

Dan was born in Goldsboro, North Carolina, on December 12, as Marine records show, but he was not born in 1949. The year of his birth was 1953. Dan was one of four children in a poor African-American family. He had three sisters; two were older than he and one, Gloria, was two years younger. Dan and Gloria were particularly close. Dan's father, Brother Bullock, worked in a Goldsboro lumberyard.

By the time he was thirteen, Dan was six feet two inches tall and weighed 180 pounds. He was a good student, enjoyed hunting and fishing, and particularly liked to run. He looked forward to the time when he would star on the Dillard High School track team.

But that time never came. In 1966, his father quit his job at the lumberyard and went to New York, hoping to get better-paying work. He did not take any of his family with him. In time Brother Bullock found a job as a factory hand making $70 a week, enough to live on but not enough to send any money back to Goldsboro.

The following year Dan's mother died, and he and his sisters went to live with relatives in Goldsboro. Brother Bullock soon remarried. He came to Goldsboro and took Gloria back to New York, but he could not afford to take the other children. Dan continued to go to school in Goldsboro, but in the eighth grade he dropped out and took a bus to New York. He was fourteen years old.

"He just showed up at the door one day," his sister Gloria remembers. "We didn't know he was coming."

Dan saw at once that the situation in New York was bad. His father, Gloria, and his new stepmother lived in a tiny, hot, dark apartment in a rundown part of Brooklyn. There was barely enough money for the three of them to live on. Dan was especially worried about Gloria growing up in the seedy tenement neighborhood.

At first Dan could think of nothing he could do to improve the family's dismal living situation. And then he had an idea. Newspapers were full of advertisements asking young men and women to join the army or marines. But a person had to be eighteen years old before he could sign up for any branch of the military service without parental consent.

Dan asked his father to sign a paper giving him permission to join the Marine Corps. His father told him no. He told him he should go back to school. Besides, Brother Bullock knew the Marine

Corps would not take a fourteen-year-old boy, even if his father gave consent.

And then, Gloria remembers, Dan was gone from the apartment just as suddenly as he had come. They did not know where he had gone or what he was doing, but now and then they had a note from him saying he was all right. Several months later he was at the apartment door again, but there was a huge difference from the first time he had come. Now he was dressed in the uniform of the United States Marines.

He had sent to North Carolina for a copy of his birth certificate and somehow had changed it—or had someone change it—to show that he had been born in 1949 instead of 1953. Big, strong, smart, healthy, and apparently eighteen, he was someone the marines were happy to have.

His father or stepmother could have ended his military career by picking up the phone and calling the Marine Corps. Dan pleaded with them not to do that. He was happy. He had finished his basic training, and he was excited about being a marine. "When I come back, I'll have my stripes," he said, and he talked about having money to finish his education.

In the face of his enthusiasm neither his father nor stepmother told the Marine Corps that Private Dan Bullock was only fourteen years old.

Before long Dan was in Vietnam. He wrote regularly to his father and Gloria. He said he was getting along fine. Sometimes he would put a money order for them in his letter. And in one letter he had written, "I don't have any holes in me."

But in early June a three-page Defense Department telegram arrived at the little Brooklyn apartment telling Brother Bullock that his son had been killed.

Someone informed *The New York Times* about Dan Bullock's true age, and a *Times* reporter called the Pentagon in Washington, D.C., for details. After a quick investigation, the Defense Department acknowledged that Dan had altered his birth certificate, that he had enlisted at age fourteen and was killed at age fifteen. The Defense Department announcement said that Dan Bullock was the youngest serviceman killed in the Vietnam War and might have been the youngest killed in action since World War I.

A *New York Times* reporter went to the Bullocks' Brooklyn apartment to get information for a story. When he left he saw Gloria Bullock sitting alone on the tenement steps. He reported in his story that he had heard her say to a visitor in a tearful voice, "He shouldn't have died. He joined to help us out. He shouldn't have died."

With the help of her brother Dan's life insurance money, Gloria finished high school and went to Kingsborough Community College in Brooklyn. She studied business education and today works in a bank in Newark, Delaware.

When I talked to Gloria about Dan, she repeated the words she had spoken that day in Brooklyn more than twenty-five years ago.

"He did it to help us out," she said.

Lt. Colonel Anthony Cameron Shine. He is holding his flight helmet but wearing his lucky "hundred mission" hat. Since 1980, the air force has given annually the Lieutenant Colonel Anthony C. Shine Award *to a young fighter pilot who most exemplifies Lt. Colonel Shine's exceptional level of proficiency and professionalism in flying a tactical fighter aircraft.*

ANTHONY CAMERON SHINE
Panel 1W, Line 93
Lt. Colonel, Air Force.
Date of Birth: May 20, 1939.
Date Missing: December 2, 1972.
Home of Record: Pleasantville, New York.

Lt. Colonel Anthony Shine was an air force man to the very core. A fighter pilot, he flew a hundred missions on his first tour of duty in Vietnam. Turning down reassignment to the United States, he volunteered to return for a second Vietnam tour in 1972.

"Tony was doing what he felt was the right thing to do in serving his county," his wife, Bonnie, once said.

That spirit of service and patriotism permeated Anthony Shine's family. He had two younger brothers and a younger sister. Both brothers were West Point graduates, and both fought in Vietnam. Colonel Alexander Shine, closest to Anthony in age, was seriously wounded by grenade shrapnel on his second Vietnam tour in 1969. First Lieutenant Jonathan Shine, eight years younger than Anthony, was killed in 1970 while leading his platoon; he was twenty-three years old. Sarah, Anthony's sister, was a Red Cross nurse in Vietnam.

In an interview, Alexander Shine, now retired from the army, said, "At the time of the war, particularly early, we thought what most Americans did: that Communist expansion had to be stopped. You served. I didn't spend a lot of time questioning the government. We would stop the commies."

When Anthony Shine took off from Myrtle Beach Air Force Base in South Carolina for his second tour in Vietnam, his wife and their three children—Anthony Jr., ten; Colleen, eight; and Shannon, three—were on the tarmac to see him off. Bonnie spoke to her husband through a radio hookup that had been arranged for the wives. "I told him he was looking good," she remembers.

She had also given him a note to take with him. In it she quoted the Bible, Joshua, I, 9: "Have I not commanded thee? Be strong and of good courage; be not afraid, neither be thou dismayed: for the Lord thy God is with thee whithersoever thou goest."

On December 2, 1972, less than two months after returning to Vietnam, Anthony Shine was lead pilot in a flight of two A-7D aircraft on a combat mission over North Vietnam and Laos. When they reached the target area, Highway 7, a major North Vietnamese supply route, Shine told his wingman that he was going to drop below the cloud cover to take a look. A few minutes later he reported that he had spotted a convoy on the highway and was going to attack it. Those words were the last that his wingman or anyone else heard from Lt. Colonel Shine.

When the estimated fuel time to keep Shine's plane in the air had run out and he had not returned to base, the air force ordered a search-and-rescue mission. The aerial search found no sign of the missing A-7D plane or of Anthony Shine. Like thousands of other airmen, soldiers, and marines, he had simply vanished into the dense Vietnamese jungle terrain. As it had done hundreds of times before, the air force listed Anthony Shine as Missing in Action.

The war finally ended, but for long years after that the Shine family heard nothing about Anthony's possible fate. The U.S. government said it could do nothing further to find his remains or to learn what might have happened to him. His case was the same as those of thousands of other Americans carried on the record books as Missing in Action. The government advised the Shine family, as it did all families with missing relatives, not to make inquiries or investigations on their own. Officials said it might only lead to trouble for the person if he was by some chance alive.

But like many other families with MIAs (Missing in Action) or POWs (Prisoners of War), the Shines kept pressure on the government to do more to find out what had really happened. Bonnie Shine gave speeches and organized postcard campaigns. Helen Shine, Anthony's mother, and Sarah, his sister, marched in front of the White House with signs demanding, Bring the MIAs Home. Colleen Shine, who last saw her father when she was eight years old, worked on the staff of the National League of POW/MIA families.

In 1993, a joint U.S.-Vietnam investigating team found crash and burial sites near where Anthony Shine's plane probably had gone down. They found some small airplane debris and other artifacts but not enough, they said, to make a positive identification. The case of Anthony Shine remained pending or unsolved.

Finally Colleen Shine decided to go to Vietnam herself. "If I was going to get on with my life, I had to make a final effort to learn the truth," she said.

In February 1995, she flew to Ho Chi Minh City (formerly Saigon), rented an old Russian Jeep, and hired a Vietnamese guide. They drove to the mountainous area near the Laotian border where her father's plane was believed to have gone down. Colleen found a villager who remembered the crash and took her to it and to a nearby place where North Vietnamese soldiers had buried the pilot in a bomb crater.

Colleen found small pieces of an airplane, but the stunning discovery was a flight helmet that the villager showed her; he said it was his "souvenir" of the war. He also told Colleen he had shown it to the investigating team in 1993, but that they had given it back to him. They said it had no identifying marks.

"When I looked inside the helmet," Colleen said, "I almost fainted."

There was a name inside. The ink was badly faded, but the name was still barely legible. It was her father's name.

Armed with the new and overwhelming evidence, the Shine family convinced the government to investigate the crash and burial sites again. This time, in a thorough search, they found a tip of plane wing with a serial number. The grave had been robbed, but they found one dog tag (military identification tag) with Anthony Shine's name on it. They found enough bone fragments for DNA tests. Using blood samples from Anthony's mother, sister, and brother Alexander, the Armed Forces DNA Identification Laboratory achieved a match.

In August 1996, the remains of Lt. Colonel Anthony Shine came back to the United States in a gunmetal-gray coffin. He was buried with full military honors in Arlington National Cemetery. After twenty-four years, the quest of the Shine family was over.

The cross beside Anthony Shine's name on the Vietnam Veterans Memorial has now been changed to a diamond, denoting that his death has been confirmed. But there still are over two thousand crosses on the wall beside the names of American servicemen whose fates are still unknown. Colleen Shine hopes that her family's efforts will make a difference for the many families who still yearn for answers.

Melvin Carrillo during his battalion's Hawaii training stopover

MELVIN CARRILLO
Panel 42E, Line 49
Private First Class, Army.
Date of Birth: February 8, 1949.
Date of Casualty: March 3, 1968.
Home of Record: Roswell, New Mexico.

Melvin Carrillo didn't wait to be drafted; he enlisted in the army a month after his eighteenth birthday. He had no plans to go to college and figured his draft notice would come soon anyway. He had been a good student at Yucca Middle School and a member of the Yucca football team the two years they were Roswell city champs. But he began to have trouble with his studies at Robert Goddard High School and decided to drop out. Maybe it was the idea of the draft hanging over him. Maybe it was a feeling that he ought to be out on his own. Melvin was one of ten children in a big Hispanic family; his father had always worked hard as a plumber to put food on the table, but it was a struggle. Whatever the reasons, enlisting seemed like the best idea, and Vietnam was just a word to Melvin.

The army trained him well. After boot camp at Fort Hood in Texas, he was sent to Fort Polk in Louisiana for special weapons training. Before shipping out to Vietnam, Melvin returned to Roswell to say good-bye to family and friends. During his few days there he became engaged to a girl he had known from the time he was a young boy. En route to Vietnam his battalion stopped for another thirty days of training in Hawaii.

Melvin's outfit arrived in Vietnam by ship on Christmas Eve, and all the months of good training did not help him. On January 14 of the new year, less than a month after arriving, Melvin was lead scout in a reconnaissance patrol. A land mine exploded, and he received multiple wounds. He was evacuated to Japan, then to San Francisco, and finally to William Beaumont Military Hospital in El Paso. In less than a year Melvin was back in the city where his military life had begun.

Since Roswell is only a few hours drive from El Paso, Melvin's family and fiancée were able to visit him several times. He had his nineteenth birthday in the hospital, and he was there for almost a month before he died on March 3, 1968.

Megan MacMillan took a field trip to the Vietnam Veterans Memorial with her eighth-grade class. She made a journal of her visit and sent a copy to the Friends of the Vietnam Veterans Memorial. In the journal one of the things she described seeing was a solitary rose beside a name on the black wall: John A. Jones Jr. And she wrote: "I know nothing about this man except that he used to be alive. . . ."

In those few words Megan surely expressed the overpowering message of the Vietnam Veterans Memorial: These men used to be alive.

MEMORIAL MEANS TO AMERICA • SIX:
NAM VETERANS MEMORIAL MEANS
THE VIETNAM VETERANS MEMORIAL
RICA • VIETNAM VETERANS ME
ETNAM VETERANS MEMORIAL MEANS
ORIAL MEANS TO AMERICA • SIX: W
ETERANS MEMORIAL MEANS TO AME

SIX: WHAT THE VIETNAM VETERANS MEMORIAL MEANS TO AMERICA

Since its dedication less than two decades ago, the Vietnam Veterans Memorial has won a secure place in the hearts and minds of the American people. It has sent a clear message to all veterans of the Vietnam War that their effort and their sacrifice are now understood and appreciated. It has sent the same message to all those who lost a loved one in Vietnam. It has pro-

A ROSE *of remembrance*

DURING FIELD TRIPS *to Washington, schools often leave wreaths at the memorial.*

vided a place where all Americans, no matter how they once felt about the war, can meet on the common ground of sorrow and respect for those who gave their lives.

The memorial serves as a powerful and ever-present reminder that, as a nation, we must not forget the lessons learned from the Vietnam War. One lesson is that we must resist being drawn into a war unless the security and well-being of the United States are clearly threatened. And the most important lesson surely is that it is terribly wrong to send young men and women to war without giving them our country's total support.

I once asked Jan Scruggs what he thought the memorial would mean to future generations. "I think it will make people feel the price of war," he said. "I think it will make them understand that the price has to be paid in human lives.

THE VIETNAM VETERANS MEMORIAL

is not only for adults. Children are fascinated by it, and, as John Wheeler once noted, they ask the hard questions. Who were these people whose names are on the wall? How old were they? Why did they die? Millions of children have visited the memorial since its dedication.

A MESSAGE

left at the wall on Memorial Day

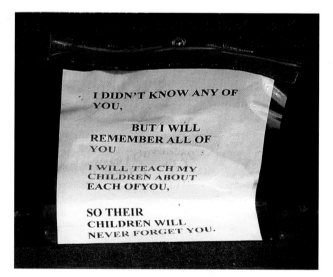

I DIDN'T KNOW ANY OF YOU,

BUT I WILL REMEMBER ALL OF YOU

I WILL TEACH MY CHILDREN ABOUT EACH OF YOU,

SO THEIR CHILDREN WILL NEVER FORGET YOU.

"I hope it will make people think about the national leaders they elect, leaders who will keep the country out of war if possible but fight it hard if there has to be war." Scruggs paused and then said, "I think the memorial will say, 'In a war young men and women have to serve their country.'"

Americans who experienced the Vietnam War or who were affected in some way by it know clearly enough what the memorial means. But the time will come when no person who visits the Vietnam Veterans Memorial will have known anyone whose name is on the wall. What will the memorial mean to visitors a hundred years from now?

I believe that the meaning then will be the same as it is today, and I agree with Jan Scruggs that the memorial will make Americans feel the price of war. The power of the memorial is in the names on the black granite wall, and they will always be there.

They will always have but one message: Any war, any time, any place, however necessary, and for whatever moral purpose, is about sacrifice and sorrow, not about glory and reward.

Jan Scruggs was twenty-nine years old when he began seriously to pursue the idea of a Vietnam Veterans Memorial, thirty-two when the memorial was built and dedicated. Maya Lin was twenty-one, still an undergraduate student at Yale University, when she conceived the design for the memorial. This great memorial might have been a fitting capstone to a career for either Jan Scruggs or Maya Lin. What does a person do when he or she has accomplished something so awesome so early in life? When the person has talent, vision, and energy, the answer is: plenty.

After the Vietnam Veterans Memorial was built, Jan Scruggs returned to the University of Maryland and earned a law degree. Today he is a Washington attorney. He has become one of America's most successful motivational speakers, with audiences ranging from AT&T staff to the Million Dollar Roundtable. He lectures to college audiences about the Vietnam War and writes articles on many topics for national publications. All the while, he has continued as the first and only president of the Vietnam Veterans Memorial Fund.

"I consider myself both an artist and an architect," Maya Lin told an interviewer in 1990. After the triumph of her Vietnam Veterans Memorial design, she earned her master's degree in architecture at Yale. Since then she has devoted herself to her art and architecture interests with outstanding success and critical acclaim. She has built houses and designed building interiors. A Civil Rights Memorial in Montgomery, Alabama; an outdoor Peace Chapel for Juniata College in Huntingdon, Pennsylvania; several imaginative landscape designs; and a number of other major works have marked her as one of the most important public artists in America today. Maya Lin has received an honorary doctor of fine arts degree from Yale University and a Presidential Design Award for the Vietnam Veterans Memorial.

FACTS ABOUT THE VIETNAM VETERANS MEMORIAL

Location: Constitution Gardens on the Mall, Washington, D.C.

Dedication: November 13, 1982

Designer: Maya Lin

Wall: The wall is shaped like a wide V, or chevron shape. Each wing is 246.75 feet (75.21 meters) long; the combined length is 493.50 feet (150.42 meters). Each wing is made up of 70 panels. Where the wings meet, the memorial's highest point, they are 10.1 feet (3.08 meters) high; they taper to a height of 8 inches (20.3 centimeters) at either end. Granite for the wall came from southern India.

Names: When the memorial was dedicated, the wall contained 57,939 names, the total of known dead or missing at that time. Since November 1982, an additional 270 names have been added to the wall, bringing the total to 58,209 as of May 1997. The names of eight women are among the total on the wall: seven army nurses and one air force nurse. The names of a small number of military persons—possibly as many as thirty-eight— who did not die in the Vietnam War were engraved on the wall. This happened because of clerical errors in the list of fatalities provided by the Defense Department. The names cannot be removed without damaging the memorial, but they have been dropped from the directory of names at the memorial.

In addition to the names, the following words are inscribed on the memorial wall:

East Wing

IN HONOR OF THE MEN AND WOMEN OF THE ARMED FORCES OF THE UNITED STATES WHO SERVED IN THE VIETNAM WAR. THE NAMES OF THOSE WHO GAVE THEIR LIVES AND OF THOSE WHO REMAIN MISSING ARE INSCRIBED IN THE ORDER THEY WERE TAKEN FROM US.

West Wing

OUR NATION HONORS THE COURAGE, SACRIFICE AND DEVOTION TO DUTY AND COUNTRY OF ITS VIETNAM VETERANS. THIS MEMORIAL WAS BUILT WITH PRIVATE CONTRIBUTIONS FROM THE AMERI-CAN PEOPLE. NOVEMBER 11, 1982.

Statue: The statue of the servicemen was sculpted by Frederick Hart. It is cast in bronze and is 7 feet (2.1 meters) high. The statue was dedicated on November 11, 1984. President Ronald Reagan was principal speaker at the dedication.

Flag: An American flag, which flies twenty-four hours a day from a pole near the wall and the servicemen statue, is a part of the Vietnam Veterans Memorial.

Important Vietnam Veterans Memorial organizations:
VIETNAM VETERANS MEMORIAL FUND
Jan C. Scruggs, president.
This organization was responsible for the building of the memorial. Among its important activities today are: (1) providing funding for renovations, improvements, and repairs to the memorial, (2) arranging and providing funding for the Memorial Day and Veterans Day ceremonies, (3) providing information about the Vietnam Veterans Memorial and the Vietnam

War to the general public. Questions and requests for information should be sent to:

Vietnam Veterans Memorial Fund
815 15th Street, NW, Suite 600
Washington, D.C. 20005
FAX: 202-393-0029
website: www.wmf.org

FRIENDS OF THE VIETNAM VETERANS MEMORIAL

Volunteers of this organization are at the memorial every day to help visitors with name rubbings, to assist in finding names on the wall and in the directories, and to answer questions. The Friends of the Vietnam Veterans Memorial has several programs available to anyone in the country. They include: (1) In Memory, which honors veterans and civilians whose names are not eligible to be on the wall but who died as a result of their service in Vietnam, (2) In Touch, a locator service that brings together families who lost someone in Vietnam with veterans who knew them, (3) Name Rubbing Program, a service that provides rubbings of names on the wall for those who cannot come to the memorial themselves. For information about these and other programs, write:

Friends of the Vietnam Veterans Memorial
4200 Wisconsin Avenue, NW
Suite 106
Washington, D.C. 20016

Allen, Thomas B. *Offering at the Wall*. Atlanta: Turner Publishing, 1995.

Ashabranner, Brent. *Always to Remember: The Story of the Vietnam Veterans Memorial*. New York: Dodd, Mead, 1988; G.P. Putnam, 1990.

Forgey, Benjamin. "Beyond the Wall." *The Washington Post*, October 12, 1995.

———. "One Monument Too Many." *The Washington Post*, November 6, 1993. (About the Vietnam Women's Memorial.)

Johnson, Thomas A. "Marine, 15, Killed in Vietnam." *The New York Times*, June 13, 1969.

Malone, Mary. *Maya Lin: Architect and Artist*. Springfield, NJ: Enslow Publishers, 1995.

Marrin, Albert. *America and Vietnam: The Elephant and the Tiger*. New York: Viking, 1992.

Marshall, S. L. A. *Battles in the Monsoon: Campaigning in the Central Highlands of Vietnam, Summer 1966*. Nashville: Battery Press, 1966.

McCombs, Phil. "Maya Lin and the Great Call of China." *The Washington Post*, January 3, 1982.

Ochsner, Jeffrey Karl. "A Space of Loss: The Vietnam Veterans Memorial." *JAE: Journal of Architectural Education*, February 1997.

Scruggs, Jan C. *The Wall That Heals*. Washington, D.C.: The Vietnam Veterans Memorial Fund, 1992.

Scruggs, Jan C., Compiler. *Why Vietnam Still Matters: The War and the Wall*. Washington, D.C.: The Vietnam Veterans Memorial Fund, 1996.

Scruggs, Jan C., and Joel L. Swerdlow. *To Heal a Nation: The Vietnam Veterans Memorial*. New York: Harper & Row, 1985.

INDEX

Page numbers in *italics* refer to illustrations.